Everything's Within

A collection of positive poetry

From a personal journey of self-discovery

by
Andrew Hawkins

©Andrew Hawkins 2020

This is a collection of poems that I have written over the past 16 years or so. When I was in my mid-twenties I was my own worst enemy, dwelling on negative thoughts of things that have happened or might happen to me. It was through constant worry that I finally had a moment of clarity in that all of these worries were just thoughts, and I am the only one having these particular thoughts, so I therefore must be the creator of them. In this realisation, and with time, I came to discover the real me that was being hidden under all this brain chatter that had taken over my life.

This led me to start writing what I call 'positive poetry'; if I can find this inner peace, then surely others can. I wanted to share this discovery, but I also found it hard to explain to people as the discovery will probably differ greatly on the person, depending on how hard they are holding on to their negative thoughts, or what many spiritual people refer to as the ego.

With poetry I believe different poems will resonate with different people and they can find their own truths within them.

The poems touch upon this discovery and the Universe we live in, and the same one that lives within us. Hence the title of the book.

We are absolutely magical if we just stop for a moment and actually realise the immensity of what we are.

There are also a handful of my more reflective poems throughout, all which helped me on my journey of self-discovery.

Thank you for picking up this book and thank you for existing.

1. Pure
2. Epiphany
4. I
5. Peace
6. Love
7. Hope
8. Happiness
9. Free
10. Now
11. Shores of Forever
12. Oneness
14. Within
15. Entwine
16. Woven
17. Sensation
18. Wish
19. Imagination
20. The Voice
22. Alive
23. Journey
24. Grow
26. The Cure
28. We
29. Shine
30. Form & Feather
31. Storytellers
32. Uncoil
33. Cycle
34. The Truth of Nature
36. Umbilical
37. Serenity
38. Strive
39. Jupiter Woods
40. Morning of Yesterday
42. Brothers & Sisters
43. Transcend
44. Spark
45. Be
46. Connected
47. Formless
48. Emanating
49. Unsung
50. Avenues of Old
51. Wonderment
52. Root & the Tree
54. I Am
55. Cosmic

56. Stardust
57. Endless
58. Euphoria's Daughter
60. Fractal Navigator
61. Eternity's Shrine
62. Eyes of the Beholder
64. Thrive
66. Star Stuff
68. Innocence
69. Inner Child
70. Reveal
71. Discovery
72. Vastitudes
74. Limitless
75. Haven
76. Anchor
77. Bone & Oak
78. Paradise
79. Reprise
80. Merge
82. Colours
83. Miracle
84. The Core
85. Bird in a Cage
86. Wings
87. You
88. Glow
90. Knowing
91. The Secret
92. Magic
93. Vibrations
94. Beyond
95. Stillness
96. Flames
97. Intoxicate
98. Listen
99. Bliss
100. Before the Fall
102. Terminal Oneness
103. Reflections
104. Rain
105. The Passage
106. Home
107. The Watcher
108. Hand in Hand
110. Veins
111. Leaves & Peaches

112. Unfold
114. Ease
115. Ebb & Flow
116. Overwhelming
118. 4th Dimension
120. The Dreaming Pillow
121. Ascension
122. Boundless
124. Axiom
126. Never-ending
127. Tracks
128. Fable
129. Infinite
130. Rainbow After the Rain
132. Celestial
133. Anew
134. Grace
135. Replete
136. Sky & Tide
138. Why?
139. Acceptance
140. Choose
142. Truth
143. Forsaken
144. Seeds
145. Unique
146. Weave
148. Essentia
150. Rejuvenate
152. Unity
153. Depth
154. Float
155. Cherish
156. Treasure
157. Everything
158. Bestow
159. Birth & Decay
160. You & Me
162. The Gift
163. Play the Game
164. Wild
165. Freedom
166. Prevail
167. Escapade
168. Inhale / Exhale

Pure

Has anyone told you that you are exactly who you need to be?

And by doing what you love you are doing enough.

You didn't come here to prove anything, you came to be you!

You are one of a kind, an incomparable masterpiece.

Yet you are part of absolutely everything.

Right now in this moment in time, you are perfect.

Never doubt your worth; you are unique and no one can take that away.

You are a conscious being of pure universal energy, that's how magnificent you are.

Epiphany

Humans grow
From new to old
And it's in this time
Our story's told

A Universal intelligence
That resides inside
With free will to feel and create

I wish for you to see
What the cosmos sees in you
Stardust evolved into form
And a heart that beats so true

To see the energy the eyes cannot
Beyond what we are told
The never ending epiphanies
Embedded in our souls

Stars die
So we can live
And cells divide
For life to give

Outside the human spectrum
And a billion books of explanations
Is the pure expression of everything
With no fear or expectations

Where peace shines from the rainbow
After joy drops in the rain
And love shines its colours bright
When the sun comes out again

I

I revere your breath, your pulse, your roots
I love you more than I can fathom
When I dream, I dream of you so free
Building bridges across this chasm

It's no secret that my feelings are true
Because they were given to me by the beauty of you
An expression of vitality played out in me
Essence of Mother Earth's divinity

That knows the day like a flower in summer
With the strength and purity of a tree
Giving out oxygen so I can be I
A body without wings but a heart that can fly

I am the forest
I am the sky
I am the wanderer
With wings deep inside

Peace

We can all go to a place inside
Where peace resides
Beyond space and time

It's not a place within our minds
But a space within our hearts

And if we stay here long enough
And listen to the beat
The one that sings the Universe
And makes our soul complete

It'll wash away the mind made woes
To those of which we cling
And remind us of our deep connection
To each and every thing

Love

From all I've come to learn in life
There's one thing that connects us all
It binds each action to the next
From atoms to stars
It permeates through every cell
Longing to survive
The very fabric woven through time
That brings our consciousness to life
It glows within each and everything
With no below and no above
The tranquil timeless serenity
Of unadulterated love

Hope

I know you're out there somewhere
Waiting for me
Like I wait for you
Staring at the sun
In a sky so blue

I know I'm in here somewhere
Calling out to you
Holding on to loves hand
In the hope it sees me through

I know I'm not the only one
Who holds this hope inside
Who is willing to share everything
And join this great divide

To know this separation
Is merely just a perception
As the Universe within us both
Fuels our inner soul connection

Happiness

No place
For old ways
Just new days
Of sensual grace

Waves they collide
Like invisible forms
Collating the energy
And passing it on

Upward and outward in every direction
In the flow of love
Passing on the Happiness
And light from stars above

Free

One Mother Earth
Never our enemy
Giver of birth
To a journey of memory

We're searching
For what we already are
Our eyes see out
From the soul in our heart

Never what we think we see
Always we, who breathe to be
The idea of ourselves
Eternal and free

Handed a piece of existence
We are our own truth
From the galaxies ablaze
Of existential proof

Now

Sleeping in a sleepless sleep
Dreaming in an endless dream
Drifting on an endless ocean
Flowing like a stream

Floating like a drop of mist
With rainbows as my brothers
Waves of intangible energy
Dancing in the light of others

Calmness overwhelms my being
Like a waterfall at dawn
The oneness vibrant like a star
Each moment from the next is born

Now has no resistance
Now doesn't have a plan
Now is your partner for life
So take it by the hand

Shores of Forever

From cell to universe
And all in between
Everything is energy
Within this conscious dream

As above, so below
Atoms collide
So the future can grow

Out of the past
The evolutionary path
Spirals forth
In the aether of now

And here we stand
As bearers to it all
Us, the Universe
One and the same
On the shores of forever
Together we stand tall

Oneness

Fleeting thoughts
Tricks of the mind
Are born inside you
And it's there they'll die

No matter what you conceive
It'll never be forever
For your thoughts are never constant
They change just like the weather

The weather may be hot or cold
Calm or in a rage
The weather never stays the same
Or lives life in a cage

Thoughts are never who you are
As they cannot be defined
And when you try to give them meaning
You get lost further in your mind

But when you can listen
Instead of answering yourself back
It's there you'll find stillness
And only your soul speaking back

The soul that shines and always has
Unquestioning, pure and bright
Which brings consciousness to life through form
Through its splendour and delight

A creature or tree accepts this gift
And gives out gifts itself
For unknowingly it knows it's one
For oneness is true wealth

Within

All around us
Above and inside us
The love within our hearts

Singing endlessly
All within us
Is where the kindness starts

There's no separation
From the truth we breathe
Or the shadows of our past

It's all perception
Of the greatest
Experience of this path

We play witness
To ourselves
Becoming what we already are

Atoms with a dose of consciousness
Ageless souls with no construct of time
Endless stars

The same song we play
Of life and love
The Universe as one

Entwine

Swimming like a star in the ocean of you
Merging our way back to the centre of truth
Radiance dawns upon our souls
And carries us on waves
Back to our home

The edge of awareness fed by the source
A visualisation of a universe shared
Between matter and energy
And the reality we dream
Of immortal synergy

Swim in me as I swim in you
In this ocean of colours that is far from blue
Carry my heart in balance with your beat
For within each breath
You make me complete

To walk the path inside your soul
To entwine like tree roots in the ground
To live in perfect unison
In this love that we have found

Woven

Sown into the dreamscape
With love woven within
Traversing through the never
Like a puppet without strings

Ignoring all the fables
Like a bud you will unfold
To become the pinnacle of self-belief
And the sower of stories told

Sensation

Experiencing the silent
Conscious revelations
The unspoken interwoven
Universal sensations

As we sail the planes
Of universal fabric
That sees all as one another
Like seedling and the flower

Opening our souls back out
From the vast cosmos within
That knows itself in the form of us
And we ourselves it's kin

Wish

Horizon to zenith
And all in between
A universe so massive
Just dying to be seen

To go back
From where we came
Is my desire
And my aim

But in my lifetime
It may not be so
But I can dream of faraway worlds
Of where I wish to go

To travel to the distant stars
To explore the corners of space
To find that we are not alone
And not the only race

Imagination

The Earth is a space station
Travelling through the black
With beings of imagination aboard
And riding on its back

Many of them do not realise yet
The grand potential of their world
That they are in fact quite magical
On their blue ball they call home

They may just be one thread in the pattern
But yet they wield the ability of thought
Which can affect all other life
When separation and greed are taught

For many yet still do not see
What they do to their only home
So I hope that evolution plays its part
And they realise they're not alone

For they are in fact part of everything
Be it water, animal or air
As all is connected deep within
When taught to love and care

The Voice

How much have you lost
When there's nothing left to lose?
How can you decide
When there's everything to choose?

In the silence of unquestioning
Every answer is revealed
In the core of every being
Is the Universe concealed

Beyond the perspective of dimensions
Between thought and feeling
Is a truth we all long for
A calmness we all yield

Many years we may go searching
For the answers to our soul
But when we stop seeking who we are
Is where all can be known

We can sing a thousand songs
Or write a million words
But none can speak the wonder
Of the nature here on earth

Formed over aeons
With a little light from the sun
Humans like ivy round this circle
Growing just for fun

Somewhere nature found a way
To think about itself
And in this moment of transition
We questioned our own wealth

But in this questioning there is a clue
That thinking is a choice
Because before all thought
Came the Universe's voice

The silent ember of existence
That pulses through our veins
That knows it's part of everything
And will forever and again

Alive

Intrigue and interest
The quest to digest
The abundance of nature
Amidst this realm of beauty

Universal wonder
Of flora and fauna
Everything before you
Is a gift

Don't get cast adrift
In memories of falsehood and fear
For they will take you away
From all this

So live for now
It's alive and breathing
From clouds in the sky
And worms in the dirt

It is the entire universe
Alive and alert

Journey

A journey back into myself
Through the vastness I do fall
Until I realise I'm being lifted
By the voice that speaks to all

The silent breath that emanates
The power that it speaks
The voice that's felt and never heard
And the truth it helps us seek

Its reverence of divinity sings to our soul
The calming undertone that knows
That you and I were meant to be
Children of seed and growth

Grow

We hear distant calls in the roots
To crawl back to our wild

We endlessly spiral forwards
To recapture our inner child

In order for us to understand this world
We must first understand ourselves

For our world exists inside us all
The one the universe has dealt

The silence of the architect
Flows freely in our soul

And in this space of reassurance
Is where we come to grow

Like the sun we rise again
To warm the shadowed hills

A sand swept ocean shore
A dreamscape of our will

Puppets who now hold the strings
Beings that know the thrill

We can wish a thousand wishes
None that may come true

But more importantly we are the wishers
The ones who can see them through

Like a waterfall we carve the rocks
That shape out over time

We are the entire universe inside us
WIth horizons so sublime

The Cure

You are the Universe
You are the World
You are the witness to all around
Experienced from within

Without your dreams
It would not be
Just the way you see
For you can change day by day
Your view of reality

You are perfect
You are divine
You are your own experience
So choose wisely with each moment
Because the choices are your mind

For every action
Sends out a ripple
With insurmountable effects

Do you choose love
Over fear that always breaks?
When your love can bend and flex

No matter the problem
It's only a perception
A preconception of fear's temptation

Can we dispel all conflict?
From our choices within
And resist all negativity
That leads us to our sins

Can we stop all war?
If our inner intent is pure
Can we heal ourselves from this?
With all our love as the cure

We

We are the sun
We are a part
Of what begun

We are the end
We are but one
Into which consciousness transcends

We are the Earth
The animals and the trees
The gift of life through birth

We are the air
Caressed in light
With endless love to share

Shine

If you could see the world through my eyes
You'd see that everything's ok
You'll feel the entire universe
Is inside you forever to stay

You don't have to be afraid
When your inside shines so bright
And you can live your life in wonder
With love your guiding light

Form & Feather

You have been alive forever
You...
The Universe in form and feather
So stay...
Stay as what you've always been
Cosmic atoms
Right now a being
A form from seemingly formless energy
Living out
The power of the stars
So be...
That of which
You already are
The pure truth of existence and breath of eternity
A wonder from afar

Storytellers

Let's leave for Mars
To terraform our hearts
To occupy a distance land
And roam amongst the stars

Let's head to Saturn
Past the moon and far yonder
And leave a peaceful pattern
Everywhere we wander

Let's become more than human
Let's reach for interstellar
Becoming beings of the Universe
The galaxy storytellers

Uncoil

The subtle elegance
Of universal intelligence
Sprinkled out everywhere
Evolving to reinvent

In the chasm of our hearts
And cascades of imagination
We generate a generation
Who will pass our love beyond

Abandon fear
It holds nothing for you here
Only make believe madness
And false sadness from our tears

The ghosts of your burdens
Fall away beneath the soil
To feed the flowers yet to come
With happiness from woes uncoiled

In the scattered leaves of a vintage autumn
The precipice of everything awaits
To lay newness into a spring unborn
As the master of your fate

Cycle

Summertime memories glide through my mind
With the birth of winter on the horizon
Autumn shades bridge the gap of cycles
Leaves fall from the spring whence they were born
The ground that was once of morning dew
Is now an ocean of fallen colours

Glancing beyond the distance
Across the blanket of nature's touch
I see you
In the glimpse of every moment
Like an art form sculpted inside my heart

The Truth of Nature

A flower blooms towards the rays
That the sun provides throughout each day
Water quenched from Mother Earth
For it to blossom and again give birth

A fox cub ventures from the den
Not knowing what or why or when
Unquestioning spirit it grows to age
At one with all on every page

The stars reflect in an owl's eyes
It does not act with great surprise
The night is one with the creature's flight
Seeing all in its magnificent sight

Small insects in millions of forms
Some working alone and some in swarms
All knowing exactly what to do
Not questioning whether there's me or you

Many creatures may hunt and kill
But they do so all for living
They do not take what's not needed
They work with what they're given

Maybe humans can one day
Remember this essential truth
That If you separate yourself from nature
You will always lose

She provides for us everything
Yet we pollute, destroy and take
I cry for generations yet to come
Please don't make this mistake

Umbilical

Trees remember light
In order for them to grow
Because growing is the only thing
That balances the moonlight glow

A forest of trees
Is no different to one alone
For all roots bind to mother Earth
Umbilical from below

Serenity

Waking up to a sky so blue
Knowing it's for me and you
Breathing the air's subtle benevolence
Letting the energy run right through

Looking up to the sky so black
Feeling the universe looking back
Living inside the Universe
The Universe living in me
An ageless infinite pact

Two parts into one
Immortal serenity
Seeing all is seeing me
Cycling through the seasons
Dispelling all the reasons
Being all I can be

Strive

Infinite expressions
Of universal succession
Time stretched out
And squashed again
To become conscious obsession

Inner observations
Of outer revelations
Ponderings of points of light
And myths and constellations

Memory's persistence
To know itself as whole
Striving for the oneness
And connections of the soul

Jupiter Woods

Glancing up as I emerge from the woods
Jupiter's glow smiling down on me
Out from the wild from where nature thrives
Looking up at connectivity

Footsteps fresh in the ground
Orange filtered leaves
Somewhere nowhere to be found
Dancing amidst the trees

Whistling hollows of a ghostly mist
Sweep my ankles like white snow
Serenity falls over all asunder
Keeping safe all that's known

Jupiter Woods, humble as can be
Trees aim towards the sky
All within is free
Shadows and light take the blame
For past which we cannot see

Can you gaze me beyond the trees?
Between the earth and the seas
The same place where you reside
In heart shape duality

Morning of Yesterday

A droplet of fleeting mist
Hangs from a leaf
A reflection of light rebounds
As in disbelief

Sunlight piercing all through the horizon
Shadows yielding to the subtlety
Of an interstellar light
Travelling with no purpose
Than to break the day from night

The crow overhead sweeps past
Like the morning of yesterday
As nature wields its beauty
Amongst the trees that sway

Sunlight piercing all through the horizon
Shadows yielding to the subtlety
Of an interstellar light
Travelling with no purpose
Than to break the day from night

Sleeping beasts rise to search the land
Night creatures go to dwell
The daylight and the sunless dark
Are not heaven and hell

They are yin and yang
Lacing endlessly into one another
Inseparable simplicity
Knowing all is sister and brother

Brothers & Sisters

Open your mind
And recognise the world inside
The truth that's a part of you
That you did so well to disguise
Everything you have is within
How long did you go without?
Focused on the outside in
Not the inside out
Now raise your hands up
Feet, still firmly on the ground
Share the joy you embody
And feel the freedom unbound
There's no more resisting
When the love keeps persisting
Brothers and sisters, always here for you listening
As one conscious family in love coexisting

Transcend

It's time to remember why you are here
The Universe in motion
Transcending love
To crush the doubt of fear
A secret revealed within your pulse
That you are life
Focus your energy on what you hold dear
At what warms the beat of your heart
If you feel deep inside
From where all connections start
You will find the spark that all life shares
Consciousness born over and over
Within every living cell

Spark

The afterglow of light that flows
Stays alight to let you know
Your existence is pure and wild
Like the breath of a new born child

The illusion of decadence
Tries to swallow the light
But the glow will shine through
Without a fight

Our natural state cannot be contained
Even through conditioning of the brain
The Universe we harbour inside
Screams out with nowhere to hide

Unquestioning and unrelenting
The burning truth
Ignites the pure spark

Falling to your knees before yourself
Surrendering to all you are
A star cast from the dark

Be

Be the flame that ignites the bond
And be free like fleeting embers
Be the water that carves a stream
That safely floats your dreams

Be autumn leaves that dance in the wind
Above a carpet of moss
Cast across the forest floor
To guide you when you're lost

Be the kindness that drowns hate
Be grounded like a tree
Be the love that connects us all
So everyone can see

Connected

Leaving the world behind
I see the way I can
And when I say the world
I mean what's gone before
And all that's in my mind

The world for me looks different now
Viewed through a heart of love
No thoughts of what if
Maybe or how
Just moments filled with now

No clouds within my consciousness
No limits to my soul
A dreamscape
Of joy and wonder
Being felt as whole

No woes created from within
To misshape my heart
Just all I am
And will ever be
All connected not apart

Formless

In you I am just like me
Though expansiveness I still see
The essence in us
The truth in formless energy

Immeasurable connections
Of divine consciousness
Relentless purity
And timeless perfection

Emanating

Unravelled deep in the core
Is the Universe's precision
The change that grows from within
And wisdom of its decisions

The realisation that it is self
Underlying everything
The watcher and true wealth
Emanates throughout

Defining the laws of totality
With its every action
Ever increasing paths to new
With no concept of doubt

The aisle lays awake
Where it wanders forth headlong
Breathing in its own creation
And playing out its song

Unsung

I walk longingly and lovingly
Not worrying or with woe
Across time and nebulae
Ageless atoms being sewn

Unravelling myself untwine
From star stuff far flung
To evolve into consciousness
And sing a song unsung

To realise I am made of all
Such oneness spread afar
Learning that to be complete
Is to know we already are

For without earth
Nor space or stars
No structure would thee hold
To contain the universe within our hearts
And cosmic souls aeons old

Avenues of Old

A touch of the universe
Sweeps through your soul
Like candlelit walkways
From avenues of old

A star glittered backdrop
On a black that shines bright
That transforms all living
When day folds to night

To return where you came from
And to come back again
A being in full cycle
Across this cosmic plane

Each moment a footstep
Carried out from the heart
A vibration of love's unity
In which you play a part

Wonderment

My awareness is my freedom
And there within the truth
That I myself am endless
The leaf tip and the root

I drown myself in wonderment
And the simplicity of me
Complex in my structure
Yet connected totally

The source that binds reality
That ties all things together
That ripples between form and thought
Like the ocean feeds the weather

Root & the Tree

Heaven's not a place
It's a feeling
And it resides within your core

Beneath the doubts and prejudice
Lives the truth beyond our flaws

The mind it seeks to justify
To label and divide
But really it's just trying to learn
The cosmos oh so wide

Quite simply we are star stuff
But some can't comprehend
The vast interwoven history
Of each and everything

That we really are just energy
Fuelled by a loving heart
Which if we listen to long enough
Tells us we're not apart

For I am you
And you are me
And we are us
Root and the tree
Everything that ever was
And will ever be

I Am

I am beauty
I am strength
I am the love that never repents

I am the endless waves
That carry the ocean
I am the sound
And pure emotion

I am the darkness
I am the light
I am what's seen
And kept out of sight

I am the energy
And the space in between
I am the Universe
Beyond day and night

Cosmic

For our hearts to hear everything
We must do away with labels

That keep us separate from one another
And distance us from nature

The only thing we need to see
Is the depth beneath false walls

For we are part of the whole
Connected, pure and wild

Let's look within to an ancient source
That resides throughout all matter

That we are all a celebration
Of cosmic frequency vibrations

The silent reverberation of truth
Self-aware and beautiful

Stardust

I am that
Of which you are
Everything
That's wide and far

Knowing all
From once dark silence
I came to learn
In sound and vibrance

That all of everything
Exists within
But under our skin
We try to sunder our soul
When we let the mind take control

We meander to and fro
When we live in our mind
But the essence of joy
Is in the heart to find

Looking out
We see ourselves
As the thought of form
But a form that was born
From stardust

Endless

Join me on this journey
As our souls warp together
As we jet past innumerable galaxies
And vacuums of starry weather

Heading for the black hole
Leaving to go back home
Returning to where all settles
From the seeds that once were sewn

Euphoria's Daughter

I am everything with no name
I give my heart away
The rhythm will ignite again
For my siblings love to sway

Flowers by the riverbed
Of marsh and reed
Colouring the edges
Beauty of the seed

Clouds pass by
For the sun to expose
Itself to all receiving

Mountain high and hill top
Valleys of the mind
Snow covered fractal forestry
From seasons set in time

Beings swim on land
And graciously fly through water
Perspectives shifting wondrously
For euphoria's daughter

Silver laced rivers
Weave through the canyons
Followed by their own return
When river becomes rain

Liquid kaleidoscopic
Evanescing subatomic
Particles alive and harmonic
Creating all embryonically

The growing and the giving
Universal unison
Flora and fauna
Like euphoria's daughter

Fractal Navigator

The fractal navigator
Spirals into infinity
Visions looped upon themselves
All destinations lead to home

Riding the colours
Like a dolphin through multicoloured waves
Twisting tracks through time

Clarity becomes clear

Meandering over treetops
At one with the vibrations
Absorbing all that is beneath
To merge into spectral patterns

I blend into everything
Like a child from the womb
Born into every moment
To breathe every breath so true

To contemplate contemplation
That you are the creator
The master of the puppet
The fractal navigator

Eternity's Shrine

Claw the holographic illusion from out of your eyes
Throw out disillusion and be rid of the lies
Open the pathways leading to the sky
And revel in the glory of the sacred third eye

Feel the connection of countless reflections
Making the you that's in everything
From mountain top to atoms so small

There is no distance when the curtains come down
To reveal the trick of the system
That keeps you a fool

So veer from the footsteps
And become one with all
Wholesome and divine
In eternity's shrine

Eyes of the Beholder

I dare you
To step out of line
I encourage you
To make the most of this time
I wish you
To not be a slave
I beg you
To stand tall and brave
I urge you
To connect with your family

The whole human race

Before you lay in your grave
Wishing you could have been more
Than a drone
Day by passing day

For we are the ocean
We are the tide
We are the love
That they try to mask & hide

With televisions
And possessions
And power that divides

For we are the spirit
And we are the soul
We can still be young
When we grow old

Without worry on our shoulders
As we grow wiser and older
As we evolve
Remembering we are all
The eyes of the beholder

The fun without the fear
The day and the night
The love within the biosphere
The energy and light

We are the stars
Gazing back across the expanse
So break free from the shackles
And coalesce in the dance...

Of the Cosmos

Thrive

The sweet kiss of cosmic rays upon your face
Touches gently like a liquid embrace
Airborne energy sweeps its force
As light caresses all from a vibrant source

Flowers dance in the breeze of a meadow's shade
Untold stories of a million seeds
Growing purposely and endlessly
A hidden knowledge of wholeness permeates the ground

Intertwining earth and air
To live and flourish there

Running rivers lead to the sea
To become the ocean free
A one way journey into oneness
A cycle of harmony

Clouds form into atmospheric storms
And disperse over mountains high
Cascades of water flow again
What went before returns and never dies

Injections of successive self-suggestions
Regenerating into the next projection
Altering your minds perception
A trick of sight and preconceptions
A rush of love makes the exception
And floods inside with pure affection
Your childhood inside claims resurrection
And guides you towards perfection

The shining soul within yourself
Creating opportunities for you to grow
Light passes through the parting clouds
Dispersing the doubts you no longer show

Dream mirrored reality
Substance of subtlety
Reflecting back what the eye can see
Connections of mindset sensuality

Alive, breathing and always true
The perfection that is always you
Seeing all the beauty, feeling all inside
Stillness at the centre of all of that which thrives

Star Stuff

I live for the moment
For in the moment I live
To be all the one I can
To give all I can give

All my life
Condensed in a moment
The persistence of now

Graced by the Universe
Light passes through
Energy pulses in abundance
In the form of me and you

Unity searching back to the source
Finding a way to itself
Weaving a true course

It's only a false image of you
That hides you from simplicity
A place inside all our hearts
Of universal fertility

We are the birth and the bearer
The giver and the given
The tightest threads in the pattern
Star stuff transformed into living

Innocence

A child born with eyes full of magic
With no introduction to form
First innocent breath
And pulse of the Universe

Ready for life
Ready for all
With no sense of summit
And no fear of fall

Pure innocent and wild
Today's child not knowing
It's ready for everything
Without memories yet sewn

Being of one
Born into the physical realm
With endless conscious connections
Ready to learn it's already perfect

Inner Child

You've got to get back
Get back...
To the inner child you are
The inner child...
You've always been

It's not far

Underneath the conditioning
Of social norms
And prerequisites
Is the cosmos speaking
Telling you

That you are everything

Not some robot
Working for a system

You know you are free
So why choose not to be

You and I are all as one
So let's live forever
In an eternal childhood of fun

Reveal

Go ahead, let the blindfold slip
And reveal what's underneath
The real you that is beyond systems
And perfectly complete

You will see that fear pretends
To make you what you're not
You are human, part of nature
Not some mechanical robot

So settle now, take a deep breath
And experience all that is
Cherish this brief reality
The Universe's personal gift

To give unto you consciousness
To experience your part
To trust and treasure every emotion
That beats out from your heart

Discovery

The simple things are set in stone
No longer the need to feel alone
The beauty of this love embraced
Fills your heart where once was space

Time flies by but has no end
For now you need not to pretend
The truth that warms your inner soul
Makes you tick and now you're whole

Personal journeys of hurt and pain
The path you sailed through
To succeed and find the love inside
And find the warmth so true

An endless smile now that you wear
Your insides filled with peace
Never-ending hopes and dreams
Your loneliness released

Vastitudes

Weaving, winding
We keep on finding
New ways back to ourselves
Into which we delve

Growing endlessly
Headlong through timeless realms

Leaving which that went before
And cascading into the never
Only to find a little more
With each passing endeavour

We think that we are something else
Through concluding our deceits
Not the voice that thinks it's form
But the depth from which it speaks

A vastitude of Universes
Uncoiled upon each other
Each one born of a previous layer
Like an infant from its mother

They move in ways
To separate and reconnect
And rearrange perfection
From all knowing
To becoming

Beyond the frame of illusion
Lies pastures new
And above the pain of confusion
Is the immensity of you

Limitless

You were torn
And the pieces left in shards
You held your head up high
And battled through the scars

Dust off the shadows
And wash away the sin
You still have much to give
So let the feelings in

Shed the pain
Find room within your heart
The fear you felt not long ago
Is beginning to depart

The field of dreams that lays in wait
Will help you turn the tide
And you will soon feel limitless
With the glow of truth inside

Haven

With salty wind
We sail...
We sail to shores far beyond
To unknown lands
Yet familiar like home

A seagull feather fantasy
Mother oceans legacy
We anchor...
We anchor ashore

Abandoning our comforts
To discover everything
In a new world with no prophecies
Or autocracy
With no masters of deception
To alter our perception

We capsize our vessel
To the seabed of no return
So we can remain in this haven
And trust in what's to come
New horizons in all directions
Our hearts connecting as one

Anchor

When you're sailing
And the waves won't bring you home
Send your anchor down

Your destination still awaits
There's no need to rush around
Everything will come to you
When you turn your boat around

But when you're drifting
And the wind is nowhere to be found
Throw your anchor down

It won't be long
Until the time is right
To lift your anchor up
And sail into the light

Bone & Oak

Transpiring together this bone and oak
Enwoven trails we find
Emerging through the crashing waves
Unravelling from the mind

Sailing on the ocean blue
With ghostly mist enshrined
Traversing out into cycles old
These weathered decks be kind

No portals hold a man's prowess
To gather woes therein
These captured fish
And songs unsung
With sweat lost in the wind

A dozen days go by before
The sunlight comes to sea
With these bones weary on this oak
This boat alone with me

Paradise

Do not be guided by the waves of fear
Let the soulful winds bring you back home

Listen to their subtle calling
To sail you back to shore

On their gentle breeze destiny awaits
A paradise worth waiting for

For the tide will recede a final time
And reveal this paradise of peace

To leave a world unquestioned and pure
In which your love is now unleashed

Reprise

Show the skies
In coloured reprise
So I don't fear myself

Send me rain
And grow me flowers
And give me inner wealth

Ride the waves
Of ocean flow
And escape the pain of past

Wear my scars
And come to grow
With a love that forever lasts

Merge

When you look at the colours
Do you notice every shade?
When you see the shadows
Do you merge between the fade?
When you walk through the forest
Do you cherish every blade
Of grass that is around you
Weaving in the glade?

Don't forget that all connects you
Without the darkness, you have no light
Without the backgrounds around you
There's no definition of sight
The invisible air that surrounds visible forms
Bringing life to who breaths it
Which over time it transforms

When you look at the ground
Don't forget all above
Without what's above you
The ground holds no love
No shape to keep you stable
No truth within your eyes
As you would not be seeing things
Without the starry skies

Your own truth lies within yourself
But it's not inside alone
It's deeply connected with all around
From the cosmos to chromosomes
Make enemies at your own peril
Because your enemies are you
If you keep such hatred locked inside
You'll always end up blue

Smile at everything you see
Because everything is you and me
A billion smiles will return your way
If you love the world so free
You are star stuff captured in time
And all that's around us
Is yours and mine

Take my hand in the shadows and step Into the light
Everything will be fine

Colours

I watched you paint the colours
Across a melted summer sky
And it was in that very moment
I saw you open your wings and fly

You dotted about the evening breeze
Casting shadows on the sun
With wings of silk and a heart of joy
I took your hand and joined the fun

You showed me that to truly live
All one must do is love
So I opened up my world to you
And shone like the stars above

Miracle

I look into space and see myself
Beyond black holes and through the shelf
I fly everywhere between the fold
Of space and time
And stories untold

I fleet between dimensions wide
And landscapes old
To continue stories for another age
Where conscious pathways
Never cease to play

I traipse through stars
And wade through galaxies
To bring myself home
Aware of what has gone before
And all that is yet to be

For the ocean of us is a miracle
A joy to comprehend
That every single atom
Of every single thing
Is connected

The Core

Distant fires in the sky
Seen through my being's eyes
Blackness illuminated
In the light of disguise

A place beyond imagination
But where imagination is from
A scene of external existence
In an ever freeing freedom

Like the wings of a bird
I cut across skies of atmosphere
Gracing a background of clouds
Ascending on love, leaving fear behind
A blue sky painted with hazy shrouds

The core of everything stems from oneness
And thrives beyond the visual surfaces
As the end of time loops back on itself
And conjoins to make our reality
Of strength, beauty, depth and frailty

Bird in a Cage

Imagine, if you will, for a moment
That you are a magnificent bird
Now imagine again that you're in a cage
And just think if you were born that way
You'd have nothing much to say
You'd accept it as the norm
And never wish to fly away

Now imagine again if you will
That government is the cage
Does this not set in motion thoughts
That the cage is just a stage?
One in which you are controlled
And with nothing much to say
For you were born into this cage
And you guess that's just ok

The truth is the cage is not for you
It's of course for them
For without said cage there's no control
And all that's left is your freedom

Wings

Life is like a butterfly
Free spirited and wild
We stop occasionally in awe of its delights
And fuel our inner child

These moments are everywhere
In each and every beat
So taste them all and live your life
With wings beneath your feet

You

You
Must see
What you already are

The truth
The Earth
A flight around the Sun

You
Will see
If you open up your heart

Your life
Your soul
As one with all so whole

So leap
Into
The endless abyss of you

Glowing like a billion stars
And shining oh so true

Glow

Billions of beings visible from space
The creators of their own light
After aeons of transformation
They shone in the night

An alien's eyes cast down upon
A misty blue and green
But on the far side of the sun
Glow cities like a dream

Little do they know of our battle down here
A fight amongst each other
When it's easier to share

The only lesson we need to learn
Is the one about us
That we are what the Universe created
Just how it intended
Its oneness extended

A freedom of expression
In our passion
It comes crashing
Down over fear

A freedom of expression
A love transgression
Of energy patterns
Dancing round this sphere

Knowing

As my fear slips beneath the soil
I leave behind my woes and toil
To live a life in love's devotion
Fulfilled with promise and pure emotion

With each breath I'm born again
Into acceptance and ecstasy
Knowing that when our hearts met
It was unsheathed destiny

The Secret

Thoughts spoke to me through distorted static
Hiding the colours, keeping me in a panic
I borrowed its face
To create one of mine
I tainted my being
And stepped away from the divine

My journey was hopeless
A fool returning to the same place
Of burdens and watchmen
And I cried out in shame

I touched upon a secret
That was always nestled there
At the core of everything
My own universe lay bare

I looked down upon myself through humbling light
Shining my colours when I was lost in the fight
I came to my senses
And carried myself all the way
To the place I had hidden beneath imagined sheaths
Emerging like a new sunrise
Rising above mind conjured beliefs

Magic

If you could see yourself
How I see you
There'd be no more sadness
In a world you turned blue

There would be more colours than a rainbow
And endless joy that's overdue

A carpet of bluebells
And a picnic for two

And no more shadows
Cast down upon you

Just a world of which is magic
Where birds sing out your path
Wave goodbye to all that's tragic
And feel the love that fills your laugh

Vibrations

Many claim that they are lost
When we are all at home
In the Universe so beautiful
Where nothing is alone

Connected by the finest threads
Of energy vibrations

Whatever your form
Wherever you may be
I love you without question
Because I know you are me

Beyond

Are you awake?
Or is it a dream?
Is this existence of reality
Just what it seems?

Is it just wavelengths?
The ones we perceive
Or is it beyond form
Where reality leads

For what of our senses
That haven't evolved
To see spectrums beyond
And hear sounds of old

To see all of the patterns
Our awareness on fire
To feel every atom of the universe
Beyond earthly desires

Stillness

Fade out, erase
Your mind, your ways
Your ego of you
Separate and untrue

Your mind is fiction
It tries to conceal
The glory of you
Your existence so real

We are children of the stars
So live your life like nothing less

You think you don't have a future
And you're right I must confess

All you have is this moment in time
And in this moment you have everything

The chains of time hold no power
Against this stillness deep within

Flames

Lost within your soul cage
No distance to the edge
Remnants on another page
Your own self to pledge

Time scales of illusion
Space dust playing games
Elements charged by the stars
Vibrating from the flames

Fragments of reality stretch
Into the retrospective of disguise
A diversion into consciousness
Pure magic brought to life

Intoxicate

And so the transformation begins
Metamorphosis of human beings
Consciousness spiralling endlessly
Webs woven within themselves

The door to the Universe
No longer needs a key
Feel the shackles fall away
Pure light intensity

The love that you held on for
Now holds you in esteem
Embracing you as just the same
In this intoxicating dream

Listen

Do not confine yourself to the sounds in your mind
Listen to your heart and see what you find
There may be a rhythm, there may be a beat
That's the sound of your energy, true and complete

So don't let the mind cloud this purity with woe
Tune into your heart and live life with the flow
See the connections in everything that is
And enjoy your existence in this state of bliss

Bliss

When the sky drops
I'll be there to give you shelter
When the sun stops
I'll be there to light your dreams

When the light that gives
Fades out from a distance
I'll carry the energy in my heart
And reignite the beams

When the Earth stops turning
When shadows move no more
When time has no more meaning
I'll be waiting by the shore

When the sands of time stop falling
When the nights become the day
When the sounds turn into silence
A new sun will light our way

Pure light that's felt by all
The cosmic ocean's gift
A pathway to pastures new
A leap forward into bliss

Before the Fall

Do we need a reason to live?
When living is reason enough to give
Just by being here and sharing you
You keep others from being blue

The Universe gives before it drifts away
In every fragment of its fold
Energy passing itself on
Before its story is told

Lights of creation fire up the dark
To illuminate the cosmic spark

But before their final fade
They lay their contents across the shade
To become children of one's self
The very same of which it's made

If we look outside for answers
We are looking at our past
For everything we have come to know
Lives presently through our hearts

But if we dare to look inside
We will see reminders of who we are
Universal awareness
Descendants of the stars

Some may say it's magic
Others may not understand
But every conscious perception
Is part of the oneness so grand

The song of the Universe
Sings freely within us all
So let's join hands across the Earth
And give everything before we fall

Terminal Oneness

Distractions of a physical realm
Of which the body dwells
It is not separate from the soul
As it is witnessed there
And there alone

Not apart from any other
For the same realm is our mother
Mother Earth she thrives inside us all
With each breath we shine

In each moment
We live as reflections
As the Universe's offspring
Growing to connect

There is nowhere to hide beyond our form
Only truth that sees beneath what's born
A successive connection of heritage
Cosmic injected beings
With souls for all adorned

Terminal oneness
Our destiny speaking from the light
It's been calling our name forever
Telling us we're not alone

Reflections

Capturing sensations in the moment
Painting a scene so serene
Reflections in the wishing well
Of blue, white and green

Light leaves the rainbow on
To shine its colours when the rain has gone

Moon crest chases the sunset

The backdrop of naked stars
Soar in the night sky
Lighting a track
Into every human eye

Droplets of burning beauty
Swimming on the wings of blackness
Through invisible substance
With no destination

Trapped in euphoria

The continuum of presence
Bound to the boundlessness
Interwoven energy far and wide
Condensed in a tear drop that I can't hide

Rain

Erase the phase of past dark days
Emerge from beneath the mire
The setting sun helps guide you home
To that which you desire

The night crawls in
As broken clouds cry
Cleanse yourself with moonlit rain
Sent earthward from the sky

Tears of joy hide on your face
Dancing with drops of rain
With arched back and open arms
This paradise you now obtain

A graceful descent onto your knees
You watch the waving ocean
Taken by the hand of love
The most transcendent emotion

The Passage

We built our walls
And knocked them down
We burnt our flags
And turned around
Today's a different day
Another realm
Where we can stay
Where all are loved

No soul left behind
A family of beating hearts
Unquestioned by the mind

Our tale is told
And grows forth
From stories of old

The passage that brought us here
Was a lesson learnt in time

And now we stand side by side
To take this story to the grave
Of the ones who loved
The ones so brave
The ones with peace written on their sleeve
With the world to serenade

Home

I am the choice of myself
With every decision I grow
Every part of my experience
Reminds me I'm already home

Transpiring that I already am,

Love

Life
And
The consciousness of existence

My journey is already complete
And all I have to do is live it

The Watcher

One day I'll walk into the forest
Never to return again
But I will still be here for you
To ease you from the pain

Shining in every sun ray
Fluttering in every leaf
Sparkling in every star
Sending my love to ease the grief

I'll be watching over mountain tops
And smiling from the moon
To make sure that you're ok
In this life that's gone too soon

Hand in Hand

I used to sleepwalk through the day
My dreams at night were real
Until I put life on display
And realised I could feel

Tantalising shifts in space
Surging wild purity through my veins
A galactic scene played out for me
A moon mirrored ocean that set me free

My picture hanging on the wall
A painted reality that subsided
Destiny that gently pulled the tide
Into swelling reflections that love can't hide

Lighting a fire to make the night pass by
Watching the sunrise play out in our eyes
Tomorrow we will reminisce
A promise of another yesterday
With a tender kiss

All life chanting from the heart
Waking up our dreams provide
A story in which all are a part
Standing hand in hand
Side by side

We are the festivals of natural chemicals
Created from a storm
Replenishing our paths anew
Particles of the universe reborn

Veins

This passion coursing through my veins
That once was pain but now is freedom
Between my weathered skin and bones
This togetherness has bound my feelings

The many dusty roads I've walked
The withered faces I've seen
I thought it was all for nothing
But now I know what it all means

I was searching for that missing something
Not knowing what it was
But it's found its way into my life
Without it now, I'd be lost

The missing piece of the jigsaw
Has put itself in place
And every fibre in my being
Flies free and speaks its grace

Leaves & Peaches

Why do so many
Take the long way home
Not realising
Home is here within

For we expand and thrive
Like leaves and peaches
Until
We fall where we grow

But some of us
The lucky ones
Get picked and tasted
For a brief instance of eternity

We pass our presence onto others
The sweet nectar of our souls
Appreciated in a moment
We nourish and nurture

And blend into the glorious abyss
Of space, love and time

Unfold

Your perspectives are boundless when free of fear
The fate of your awakening to all that's near
We're taking you home
To the only place we've ever known

The place where you and I can touch the sky
The sanctuary that lives beyond the eyes
The haven that thrives when stars collide
The sanctum from which you were born inside

For this eternity was given to you
The gift of yourself in each moment new
Translucent landscapes far and wide
Nowhere to which you can run and hide

Have you smiled and looked straight back?
To see the love you hold
To see completely who you are
To let yourself unfold

Reaching out to all you know
Letting go of all that's gone
Atmospheric floods of joy
The universe to expand upon

Nature's way of knowing form
For you are it and it adorns
Aware of the self-awareness
From life that was and yet unborn

Ease

Come with me ye youthful soul
Into the light of radiant meadows
And the return of yesterday
Cavort with me in the afterglow
In the warmth of burning sunsets
And the chorale of trees sway
Laze with me in the slumbering oaks
Until the sky turns an amber haze
And we rise to the morning hymn
The horizon paints a new day forth
With a breeze to ease the heart
And a new realm in which we swim

Ebb and Flow

Beauty surpassing
All that you held to be true
In this limitless horizon
In the truth that is you

Gasping with each breath
With toes in the sand
The sun bathes us gently
As we walk hand in hand

The ocean plays our song
The one of true love
As a heart shaped cloud
Passes over blue skies above

The tide never ceases
It ebbs and it flows
Just like my love for you
That continues to grow

We shape each other
Like the waves carve the shore
A reunion of the Universe
Its sentience in our core

Overwhelming

Imagine a piece of dust
To the size of the Earth
Well that's the size of the Earth
Compared to the Universe

Overwhelming Splendour
Unknown in size
Too much beauty
For mere mortal eyes

Gas giants and stars
Nebulae afar
Teasing our telescopes
We amaze and wonder

Galaxies and black holes
Supernova's so bright
So much more out there
Than the black sky at night

Where does it end?
Is ours the only one?
A Universe so grand
Too much to fathom

I long for answers
That may never come
To know why and how
How did it become?

But I can live being humbled
By intergalactic elegance
Dumbstruck by billions of galaxies
Floating across the Universe in their own little dance

4th Dimension

Full speed into the headwind
Breaking the speed of light
Pushing on through new boundaries
Until the past is out of sight

Touching on the unknown
Grasping new sensations
Knowing all there is to know
Breaking into the 4th dimension

Sparks of reality left behind
Echoes trailing in your wake
Sailing on the winds of time
As change unwinds and escapes

Your ideals all washed ashore
No longer longing for disclosure
Everything you need to feel
Is inside and around you

Your peace of mind
Your third eye blind
Blinded by the starlight
Pure white and shining bright

Destinies of ecstasy
Heartfelt pure sanctuaries
The temple within
Shines light like a billion fireflies

Far away yet deep within
Knowing all is already known
Drifting endlessly amidst the stars
Cavorting in your one true home

The Dreaming Pillow

Softly, slowly, I lay my head
Upon thy dreaming pillow
Dreamscapes flow into my being
Beyond what can be spoken

For what waits is nothing but heaven
Deeper in the hollow I drift
Soaring to join the light at the centre
What I'm feeling is a gift

Drifting on the dreaming pillow
Floating down this utopian lane
Lakes of love and rivers of peace
Beyond my thinking brain

Straying from the dreaming pillow
Taken by the stirring rouse
I awake from my tranquil slumber
Gone in which are hours

The timeless presence
Of a place behind drawn eyes
A reality without question
We can bring into our lives

Ascension

It's one's imagination
That drives the world outside
It's only false fed fear
That keeps you in the lie

So go to where your mind desires
And create your dream's intentions
There's no need to suffer
When you are the Universe in ascension

Evolving to understand itself
Just be yourself and thrive
As the one divine consciousness
Ever present and alive

Boundless

Sons and daughters of a sunlit sky
Driven to their knees by a mind of lies
But the truth in their tears as they cry
Reveals the love that cannot be denied

The ascendance of our descendants
Flow through our veins
From ashes and remnants
Evolving to cascade

We find ourselves in one another
Existence existing within itself
Like rain drops cast from a cloud
Returning back when they hit the ground

And those who live their life in love
Will catch the waterfall
And lift the sick to their feet
Because nobody should crawl

Equality entrenched through adaptation
A DNA manipulation
Of universal psychedelic apparitions
That pave the way for new decisions

A vision inside a memory
Waits no longer now
To guide our future into the past
And shape our beautiful world

Now let's stay here astounded
Transmitting our love so boundless
Travelling on a blue space island
Lighted by the sun's fluoresce

I love each and every one of you
Just the way you are
And the power of our smiles
Connect us from afar

Axiom

Something in the energy
Calls my name
And it knows more than anything
That you and I are the same

It does not dwell
But is always there
Pervading everything
Open and ready to share

Some treat it like a secret
Some say it's deep within
It reverberates throughout all that is
And if you listen it does sing

The song of everything
Harmonious in its nature
For without there's no within
And within there's no without

The axiom of you
Is the same as me
All is existence
All of it is free

In every breath
Every drop of sweat
In every action that ever was
It sings on with no regret

For all of its pastures
Will live on and on
In the growth of everything
In this never-ending song

Never-ending

There's no need to fight when you can teach
No need to stretch when you can't reach
It'll come when the time is right
When the light of day blends into night

And even though thy weary soul
May burden itself with woe
Those woes are generated from within
And can be the seeds of growth

For the love we all hold within has no limits
It's free and never-ending
So I choose to give it endlessly
As long as the days and nights keep blending

Tracks

I'm building bridges so the river flows
I'm passing through the depths of time
Where only love is known

I'm glowing on the riverbed
Like a star for you to find
And like the water that always flows
The love you give is mine

I'm breathing in my destiny
Escaping to come back
Returning to a place that has always been
At the end of every track

Fable

Lay me down in fields of old
So in centuries to come
My tale is told

To share my story throughout time
An endless fable
True and divine

One that tells of what's to come
And what has gone before
That we all are one

A shared Universal consciousness
In an endless cosmos
Of fun

Infinite

If I left this world tonight
I'd be back tomorrow
With your universe in my heart
And my soul free of sorrow

I'd journey there and back again
To play the music of the stars
To recognise myself in your eyes
And end back at the start

Rainbow after the Rain

You're somewhere far
Yet inside me
Long but not lost
A dream beyond the sea

Miles are no distance
When intentions have their way
Like dreams they float endlessly
In their own aerial ballet

As we spiral round and round the sun
Our love remains as one
Pure energy unseparated
Since time once began

Emotions of the notion
That one day our forms will entwine
The sweetest love potion
That one could ever find

I don't need a reason
To fall in love with you
But you have given me many
And my veins they course right through

Just one touch
One gentle kiss
To hold your hand
I long for this

But until that time
In my heart you'll remain
My love, my one true love
My rainbow after the rain

Celestial

And those emotions doth rise and fall
Upon this open plane
In the vastness of the void
Whence heart doth conquer brain

Be it so that truth be known
From ripple and cast stone
This change cometh through endless time
Within blood and throughout bone

Form bestowed celestially
Luxurious patterns thou weave
Thy energy passes on and on
A path of serenity paved

Lights raining from the sky
Beam forth through sensory bliss
The frontier of new dreamscapes
In which we're all a part of this

Anew

Underneath the arch of the rainbow
The rain and tears collide
In a collision of pure joy
Across the great divide

The misty grass between your toes
Connects you with the earth
Reminding you that one and all
Is death as it is birth

The cycle of the Universe
Will ebb as it does flow
Giving way to forms anew
As evolution grows

To taste this fleeting moment
As we exist amidst this plane
Is a pure gift of existence
Like a rainbow in the rain

Grace

Sometimes the colours
Form an arch in the sky

Sometimes the clouds part
To have the Sun as their eye

Sometimes the river becomes the sea
And sometimes the ocean crawls back to me

Sometimes we catch our breath
In icy winter air

Sometimes we gaze up
And the stars make us aware

They are the givers of all life
Spread across all space

Forming life over time
We are the holders of their grace

Replete

When the sky falls into me
I'll be all I can be
Part of the unfolding cascade
Sent back to the cosmos
Still part of the ever growing tree

We are never complete
With ground beneath our feet
It's just an illusion of the journey we are on
A path to which we all belong
Connectors to all that's replete

In us all is all that is
Outside us all we can be
The surroundings of all to come
And the internal moulding to which we will succumb
The promise to be free

Evolving to know we are the cosmos
Consciousness created to discover its own design
Thinking for itself inside
To realise, everything is connected
And harmoniously combine

Sky and Tide

It's time to remember why we are here
The Universe in motion
Transcending love
To crush the doubt of fear

Like a satellite in flight
Your love sails around the globe
Touching everything
Should you set it free

To give is to receive
So why bring forth hate?
When we are life
And the mind's eye light

Lighting up our connections
That are sparked out of oneness
We see wonders wide
Of a tale aeons old

And the tales that are told
Be they truth or lie
Will ripple on through consciousness
And through the sky and tide

So speak your love
And live your peace
To give meaning
To an ancient fact

And we will see everything
That we are the same harmony
Of the Universe around us
That has come to life within

Set in action by our love
From our words and actions woven
The threads of every heart
Will speak a truth unspoken

Why?

Why do I feel so free?
Is it to do with what's inside of me?
Love, joy and divinity
Experiencing a small part of eternity

Inside the energy unbound
My place in time that I have found
A body that feels, a mind that knows
A heart that loves and a soul that grows

Contemplating conceptions
Of thought patterns and deceptions
Glowing in the array of my neurons
Absorbing the reality of reflections

Why do I feel so free?
Could it be the "I" inside of me?
The being I am, emanating vitality
A cognitive mind, refining reality

Acceptance

Accept yourself for who you are
No matter what comes your way
You are life, you're wonderful
Let perspectives fade away

Alive with every breath
Every moment you can change
To become the best of you
And the master of your ways

Be thankful for this chance
To lower false defences
To capture all the light inside
And live at one with your senses

Choose

I am a fiction
Of many facts
A universal engine
With a soul contract

I am a growing seed
Interwoven into everything

I am seen as a form
Beneath which all is energy
Defined by my actions
Yet formless at my source

We see love and fear as reminders
That positive and negative are dividers
We see them as what can and cannot be
Yet we are both of them
We just choose which one to see

Both are witnessed from within
Deep beyond our walls
Do we choose to live in darkness?
Or love and share with all?

At the centre of all is balance
In the core where all is seen
But you alone can tip the scale
If you choose to love just being

Truth

Paving the way to make space for this
Absorbing the light that gives us this
Hearing the sounds that call with bliss
Breathing the air's gentle kiss

Rhythms in a heartbeat
Reflections in the glass
How many people see the truth?
Beyond the human dance

The expression from inside
Like a soldier laying down his gun
When the fear of death lets go its grip
When love conquers the numb

Masquerades of another shade
A party with no masks
A destiny not far away
In a world where freedom basks

Forsaken

The time forsaken is ours
Too late to forge in stone
Apples from the apple cart
New seeds to take us home

No ink within the manuscript
Just stars to call our own
A winged horse to carry us
To a land of flesh and bone

Forming from the formless
With a spark of light our guide
We unravel from the darkest dark
Old souls we need not hide

And float we do across the void
The fathom and the wide
To become that which we've always been
The Universe on high

Seeds

The seeds of our mantra
Played out in form
Holographic vastitudes
Fascinating and warm

Beyond the edge of infrared
Waveforms projected beneath the eyes
Spectrums that enrapture
Discoveries that dazzle and mesmerise

Secretory activity of the pineal gland
Touching upon hidden destinations
We watched the fear demise
In a love filled dimension

In a place where we are neither dead or alive
Quintessential visions like a gift
Through billions of miles of darkness
To sail through trails of a galaxie's drift

Like an autumn leaf frolicking through crisp air
We rippled through a velvety ocean of stars
Transpiring on the other side
Interlacing into all from afar

Unique

Are you thankful for the morning light and starry nights?
Are you thankful for the one chance you have, to be uniquely amazing?
Are you thankful that you were given a life, and life was given to you?
Feelings to connect and a sky so blue
Sounds and sights purely abundant and true
One life, one journey, one gift of you

Weave

Absorb the light
The gift of life
Invisible waves of ecstasy

The green trees
And ocean blue
The air that you breathe

All you are
From newborn
Is internally free

Choose your path
The one inside
And intrinsically weave

Cherish each moment
As we live for now
Bury all that burdens you

Be all you want
Driven by desire
Let your senses through

Guide yourself to pastures new
The past holds only clues
To the wonder you can become
And all that makes you true

Essentia

Absorbing the love from out of the sun
Then giving it out so no one has none
The sharing of your essentia
Will break all of this dementia

To disconnect, reject, object
Casts a lonely pool in which you swim
A pool full of your fears
Alone in which the light shines dim

To swim free like a rippling tide
To accept, acknowledge and to shine
In a world with no corners
And no dividing borders

Integrating, mesmerising
No more hiding or disguising
The grace of you
Benign and true

Roots of singularity entwining and blending
Can you feel the love ascending?
Washing over all receiving
Acceptance in stillness, alive and breathing

When our minds are reversed
Our hearts will traverse
Into the realm that adorns,
Oneness into all that's born

Rejuvenate

We watched you lay concrete over green
Making false profit from dead forests
Like a cold hearted machine

You lit our fires of passion inside
To protect and cherish our mother
On which we all reside

Your artificial systems will crumble
As nature takes over and shines
Leaving your empires to tumble
Back into the divine

And you'll be the ones to witness fear
For your actions and done deeds
But through our reaching hands
And open hearts

You will see that you are loved
When we lift you off your knees
You are only human after all
And we learn from our mistakes

In our forgiveness
We will wither away the madness
Replacing your fear with unconditional love
And rejuvenating kindness

We'll celebrate each other
We'll harmonise this sphere
Our birthplace of wonderment
In this universe so dear

Unity

Show me your dreams
And come swim in mine
I'll dance endlessly in them
Until the end of time

Lend me your heart
For eternity
And I'll give you mine
And together we'll see

Everything our souls desire
And beauty they unfold
A unity so sacred
Living young until we're old

Take my hand
On this treasured path
And walk by my side

I'll take you everywhere
You long to go
With love as our guide

Depth

My heart was once an unread book
With secrets to reveal
A depth of which was bottomless
But now it's read
I have peace of mind
And nothing to conceal

Float

Meditation for medication
Not indoctrination for a nation
Chemicals of a brain made kind
A cure through vibration
Wash away the excess mind

Visions of being
Ethereal peace through and through
Empathic pure synchronicity
Bringing yourself back to you

Hold still and take your time
Captivate the soul inside
Be the only place you'll ever be
Inside yourself where you reside

Empathic pure synchronicity
Bringing yourself back to you

Breathe lightly on the gentle breeze
Weave between the emotions
Float away amidst the trees,
White mountain tops and oceans

Cherish

What is sacred?
What's old from new?
What is underneath?
The thoughts that lead us away from truth

Could fear be masking
If we keep on asking
Unnecessary questions of ourselves

I believe if we just accept what is
Then the burdens lift
And sets fear adrift

Opening up the waves of love
For us to lead our lives brand new

And cherish every moment
Every breath
And live our lives so true

Treasure

I'd dive into the centre of the sun
To alter time's persistence

I'd build a universe inside you
To show you love conquers all distance

I'd write a song with no words
From one heart to another

Like a ray from the sun
Breaking through cloud cover

I cannot sleep under broken stars
For all connect, we are a part

To fix them I'd take every risk
With no fear to stop my love

As in your eyes I see everything
Your soul a reflection of me

The only treasure that I desire
Parts of the wholeness we're destined to be

Everything

We are the world
The Universe uncurled
An imagination of ourselves
Creating what comes forth
Out of which that went before

Through our minds we imagine thus
Of what our hearts desire
To paint a world
Where we wish to dwell
For a moment in eternity

Hand in hand
And heart in heart
Beating with beauty
Knowing you're everything
And with every ending a new start

Bestow

Your love is as soft as a whisper
As light as a breeze
As strong as a storm
Ever circling me

I couldn't have wished for a greater wonder
You've bestowed unto me
A love like no other
That breathes effortlessly

This harmony in each moment
That I am ever thankful for
Keeps my heart beating
And my soul energised evermore

Birth & Decay

The sound of leaves
Makes me believe
In trees of serenity

The colour of autumn
Wraps around my heart
And reminds me of home

And the ever flowing connections
Of birth and decay
Endlessly feeding each other

Knowing nothing is alone

You & Me

Conspiracies are another distraction
To divide us further through reaction
Let us deal with what is real
Mother Earth she needs our action

Please wake up
Get off your knees
You have everything within you
To stop this true disease

The fact that we are powerless
To those that hold the power
To do whatever they like to Earth
Hour after hour

A day will soon come, if nothing is done
When money shows its true worth
Because we won't be able to eat coins and paper
When there's nothing left on Earth

It's easy to think it's not my problem
But what about generations to come
If you were in their position
You'd wonder what they've done

To leave to you a dying world
All because of human greed
It's not money that makes the world go round
It's you and me

The Gift

Do you really need everything?
That they say you need
To lead a better life

Will you truly be happier?
Once you've voted and taken sides?

Every empire that has ever ruled
Is an empire that has fallen

Because you cannot contain nature's nature
And its desire to be free

For every abandoned city
Is now overcome by trees

If trees can grow where their seeds fall
Why can't we do the same?

To live freely and in harmony
Instead of being a name

Do we need to be treated like children?
When we are fully grown

Play the Game

You think that you are ordinary
No exceptions for the way you feel tonight
A pathway to another story
Visions that you thought were out of sight

The shadow of your shelter looms outside
Too fearful that you'll never be the same
A lost hope in the darkness wanders
Breathe in and play the game

A weight upon your shoulder burdens
When daylight turns to night
Returning to the sanctuary
To keep the secret out of sight

One moment in the distance
One chance left up your sleeve
Turn the tables of resistance
And see what you can achieve

The past unravels, withered and broken
Take heed and light the flame
Your hopes and dreams have spoken
Breathe in and play the game

Wild

Universal beauties dressed in skin
But when conditioned
They are distanced from the truth within

The stillness inside is always there
The purity which feels
The constantly aware awareness
The one that we all share

Vessels of love
Called back to the wild
Into the joy of oneness
As nature's perfect child

Freedom

Essence without preconception
Existence has no fear
The idea of an alternative self
Fades away into clear

Give yourself the freedom
The one you've always owned
The place you can always go to
Where peace and love unfold

Like a child that knows only play
Back in this haven
Where you are free to stay

The master of your will
And influence thereof
An ancestor of the stars
With 100 trillion cells
To give and share what you've received
Back into this realm

Prevail

Spewing forth the life from centre point
Moulded from the melting pot
Atomic scales of nuclear fusion
Now in this one small place
This one brief moment
We've fed ourselves delusion

What we are is what we've made
But the slate ahead is clean
It's up to us what it unveils
Only we can save us from ourselves
That's why when we look inside
It's only love and light that prevails

For when all have open hearts
To see nothing but the self
Confusions of past and future
Will subside into nothingness
Multitudes of oneness
Our own conscious healing suture

Escapade

Follow your heart
Into the sun
Become what you are
One who is one

A journey not walked with your feet
But an escapade with each heartbeat
Flowing back into the light that thrives
Consciousness knowing it's alive

Turn the key of positive energy
And the path ahead unwinds
The road to perfect synergy
Unravels in your mind

You are part of all that's complete
Peace and love our final feat
A connection of 7 billion beings
All one, all complete, all seeing

Inhale / Exhale

If you could only see
What resides inside of me
An untold cascade of love
And universal energy
That I just want to share
I will keep fighting love's fight
Even through the darkest affairs
I can only be true
To what I connect with inside
With no shame in my heart
And nothing to hide
So I will keep holding
My days and nights together
And wait for truth
Through endless cycles of weather
The day may never come
But I will keep breathing on
Inhaling every breath
So I can exhale them all back
To you

Find Andrew Hawkins on social media at:

www.facebook.com/AndrewHawkinsAuthor

www.instagram.com/andrew_hawkins_author

Twitter @BeardedUniverse

If you enjoyed this book please check out my other books:

Mindful Musings of a Middle Aged Bearded Man

Vastitudes

Printed in Great Britain
by Amazon

OCEAN ANIMAL SPECIES

Fact 1

Classification

Scientists sort out all living things into different 'boxes' according to what the creatures look like and what types of cells they have in their bodies.

This image shows the five 'Kingdoms' of the classification system which allow scientists to identify different forms of life. Scientists ask questions about a creature to decide which 'box' each creature needs to be in.

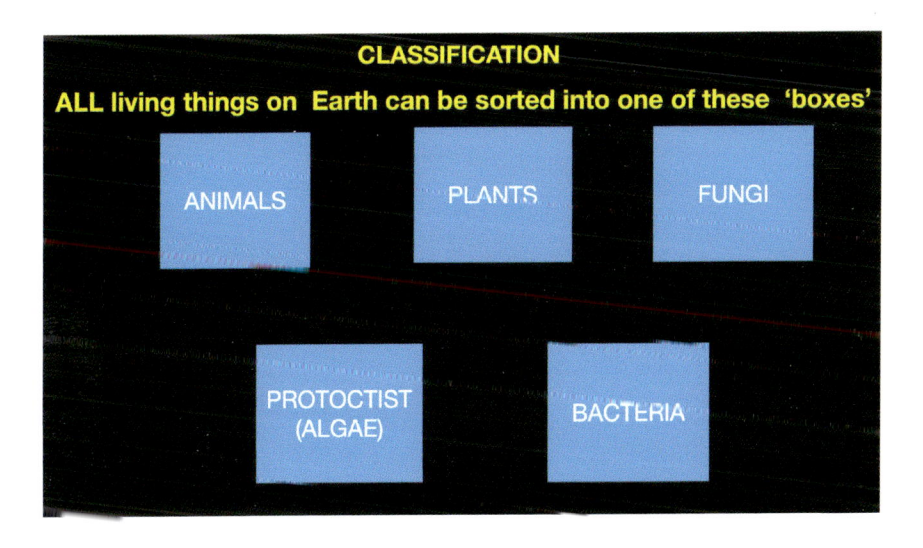

CLASSIFICATION

ALL living things on Earth can be sorted into one of these 'boxes'

- ANIMALS
- PLANTS
- FUNGI
- PROTOCTIST (ALGAE)
- BACTERIA

OCEAN ANIMAL SPECIES

Fact 2

SUPER FACT
Most animals in the ocean are invertebrates (animals without backbones)

Vertebrates & Invertebrates
When scientists are 'classifying' the animals they find, the first question they ask is - does the creature have a backbone or not? These creatures are called Vertebrates (with a backbone) or Invertebrates (without a back bone).

Vertebrates which live in the **OCEAN** are fish, marine mammals (as distinct from land mammals), marine reptiles and sea birds.

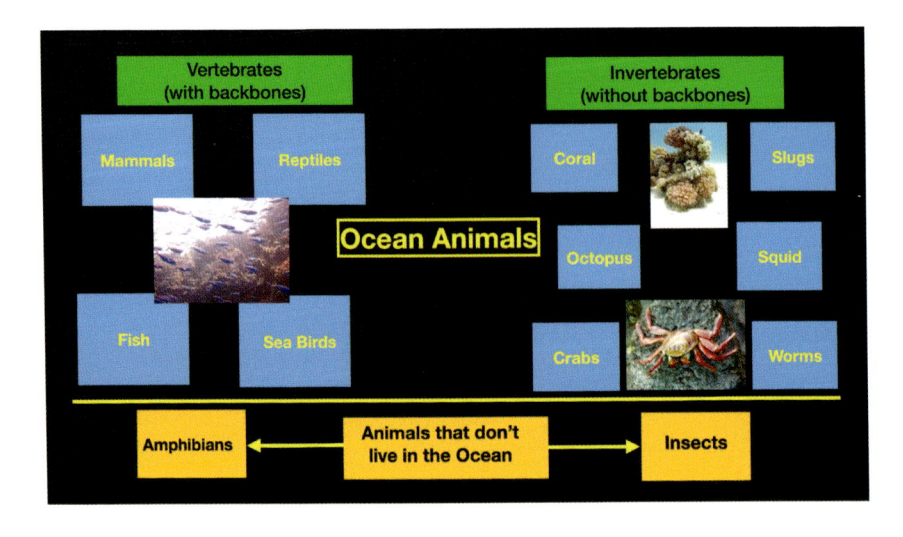

Ocean Animals

Vertebrates (with backbones): Mammals, Reptiles, Fish, Sea Birds

Invertebrates (without backbones): Coral, Slugs, Octopus, Squid, Crabs, Worms

Animals that don't live in the Ocean: Amphibians, Insects

OCEAN ANIMAL SPECIES

Fact
3

A Frog is an Amphibian
All species of animals are represented in the ocean *except* for insects and amphibians.

Amphibians only use the fresh water in ponds and lakes when laying their eggs. Once the eggs develop into larvae, then adults, they emerge from the water and live on land.

Photo Credit: David Clode on Unsplash

OCEAN ANIMAL SPECIES

Fact
4

Anemone Fish (Nemos)
All fish need gills to be able to breathe underwater.

The gills are at the side of their head and are full of thin blood vessels which can absorb oxygen from the water into their blood.

OCEAN ANIMAL SPECIES

Fact
5

Hawksbill Turtle
Sea snakes and turtles are reptiles which live in the ocean but have to surface to breathe air.

Turtles can stay underwater for up to six hours without coming up for a breath of fresh air.

OCEAN ANIMAL SPECIES

Fact
6

Sealion
Mammals do not have gills like fish, so they have to surface for air.

All marine mammals breathe oxygen from the atmosphere. A sealion can hold its breath underwater for up to 20 minutes before it has to return to the surface.

OCEAN ANIMAL SPECIES

Fact
7

Marine Iguana

A Marine Iguana is a marine reptile which lives on land but which goes into the sea to find its food. It eats seaweed and scrapes algae from the rocks with its long claws.

A marine iguana doesn't drink fresh water, so it takes in seawater when it feeds. When it returns to the land, it sneezes to remove the salt. Marine iguanas are seen with a white salt patch on the top of their heads.

OCEAN ANIMAL SPECIES

Fact
8

Dolphin
There are 42 species of dolphin, and 7 species of porpoise which live in the oceans.

Dolphins love to jump out of the ocean and sometimes spin around before falling back into the water.

OCEAN ANIMAL SPECIES

Fact
9

Herring Gull
Sea Birds are different to land birds as they get all their food from the ocean.

Seabirds normally find all their food in the ocean, but Herring Gulls now seem to spend more time on land eating waste food leftover from humans.

ADAPTATION OF LIFE IN THE OCEAN

Fact 10

Scorpion Fish

Animals in the ocean have developed both different physical and behavioural differences to aid their survival. This is called adaptation.

Adaptation such as coloured camouflage on a body is a physical difference. This poisonous scorpion fish is very clever at changing his skin colour to match the nearby similar coloured coral.

ADAPTATION OF LIFE IN THE OCEAN

Fact
11

Moray Eel
The world ocean is a massive predator-prey environment.

A large Moray Eel hides in a coral reef and eats all sorts of smaller fish, but when the tiny Cleaner Wrasse goes into his mouth to clean his teeth it doesn't swallow the little fish because it's so helpful.

ADAPTATION OF LIFE IN THE OCEAN

Fact
12

Grouper
A grouper is a large carnivorous fish that hides in the coral reef waiting to catch its smaller fishy food.

Hiding is a behavioural adaptation and physical adaptation is the camouflage of colours on the skin. Groupers have sharp teeth and chase their food.

ADAPTATION OF LIFE IN THE OCEAN

Fact
13

Shoal of Fish
Behavioural Adaptation also helps animals to survive.

Hiding in a shoal of fish is behavioural adaptation. Swimming in a shoal enables the fish on the inside to be protected from being eaten.

ADAPTATION OF LIFE IN THE OCEAN

Fact 14

Moray Eels
Moray eels are strange long fish. They come in all sizes and coloured patterns.

They usually hide in the crevices of a coral reef. There are two moray eels hiding in the coral in this picture!

ADAPTATION OF LIFE IN THE OCEAN

Fact
15

Snake Eel
Some fish look more like snakes – but this animal is a member of the eel family. It is a fish not a reptile.

This 'snake' eel hides in the sand with its head out so it can catch any little fish which pass by. Its body can be up to 2 metres long hidden in the sandy seabed.

ADAPTATION OF LIFE IN THE OCEAN

Fact
16

Surgeon Fish
Lots of animals have adapted physical parts of their bodies which help them to survive.

The surgeon fish gets his name from the very sharp fin near his tail. The fish uses his 'knife' to slash other fish so it can eat them.

Photo credit: David Clode on Unsplash

ADAPTATION OF LIFE IN THE OCEAN

Fact
17

Crab
Crabs are crustaceans. They have adapted their body to have an exo-skeleton, which is a bone structure on the outside of their bodies.

Crabs are famous for walking sideways but actually they can walk in all directions. Crabs have 10 legs. Female crabs can lay over 1,000 eggs at a time.

ADAPTATION OF LIFE IN THE OCEAN

Fact
18

Sea Urchin
Some species of ocean life have adapted poisons to protect themselves.

Ocean creatures have developed 'chemical warfare' to help in their battle to find something to eat. Sea urchins feed at night by pushing out a poisonous chemical which dissolves any living creature underneath its body. Once dissolved the urchin sucks up the fluid to eat.

ADAPTATION OF LIFE IN THE OCEAN

Fact
19

Masked Butterfly Fish
There are fish with different mouth shapes which reduces competition for food.

Butterfly fish have pointed mouths which helps them to reach algae in the cracks and crevices of a coral reef.

ADAPTATION OF LIFE IN THE OCEAN

Fact 20

Lion Fish
Lots of smaller fish are herbivores, and some large sharks are carnivores.

Herbivores don't eat other animals – they only eat plants or algae. A carnivore, like this Lionfish, is a meat eater.

ADAPTATION OF LIFE IN THE OCEAN

Fact
21

Turtle
Some creatures aren't fussy and will eat almost anything.

Turtles are omnivores – so they eat plants and animals.

ADAPTATION OF LIFE IN THE OCEAN

Fact
22

Stingray
Most rays have developed a sting in their tail.

The largest stingrays can measure up to 2 metres in length. There are over 200 different species of stingrays.

ADAPTATION OF LIFE IN THE OCEAN

Fact 23

Blue-spotted Ray
Sharks and Rays are cousins.

Sharks have developed hard fins, whilst rays have grown a wing-like body which undulates in the water to move the animal along.

ADAPTATION OF LIFE IN THE OCEAN

Fact
24

Porcupine Puffer Fish
A porcupine fish has a very special adaptation. It can puff itself up into a ball with sharp prickles on its skin.

If a fish tries to eat it, the spines hurt their mouth and they spit it out.

ADAPTATION OF LIFE IN THE OCEAN

Fact
25

Reef Shark
Sharks are fish and need gills to be able to breathe underwater.

Sharks mainly have five gills on each side of their head – but there is a six-gilled shark which lives deep in the ocean, where there is less oxygen.

ADAPTATION OF LIFE IN THE OCEAN

Fact
26

Mantis Shrimp
A Mantis shrimp has the quickest movement in the animal world.

The front legs can be used to 'punch' at a speed of 23 metres per second.

Photo credit: Roy L. Caldwell

THE LARGEST CREATURES

Fact
27

Oceanic White-tip shark
Not all sharks are dangerous to humans.

There are over 370 species of shark and most of them are harmless to humans. The job of a shark is to clean up the dead and dying creatures in the oceans to keep the oceans healthy.

THE LARGEST CREATURES

Fact
28

Blue Whale
The Blue Whale is the largest creature that has ever lived on Earth.

The Blue Whale is the largest creature that has ever lived on Earth. There are no fossils of any ancient dinosaur which was larger than the Blue Whale. The Blue Whale can only grow to its vast size because it lives in the ocean. It is the water that supports its weight. These large whales could not exist on land.

Artwork credit: Andrew Lamb

THE LARGEST CREATURES

Fact
29

Humpback Whale
Humpback whales love jumping out of the water – this is called 'breaching'. Whales are the largest mammals in the oceans.

Sperm whales dive to 2 km below the surface to hunt for giant squid. They have to breathe from the surface and often hold their breath for up to an hour.

Photo credit: Todd Cravens on Unsplash

THE LARGEST CREATURES

Fact 30

SUPER FACT
The largest fish is the Whale Shark.

Whale Shark
A whale shark can filter more than 5,000 litres of water an hour through their gills.

A whale shark is the largest fish in the sea. It is not a mammal like a whale – but gets its name from its size and the fact that it eats like a Blue Whale – only feeding on tiny krill and plankton.

THE LARGEST CREATURES

Fact
31

Albatross
The largest sea bird is the Wandering Albatross, which can have a wing-span of up to three metres.

This bird can fly around above the oceans for two years, before it returns to land to lay eggs.

Photo credit: FerNando on Unsplash

THE LARGEST CREATURES

Fact 32

Penguins
Penguins can swim at over 30 mph.

Penguins live on land but go to into the ocean to find their food.

INVERTEBRATES

Fact
33

Hard Coral Polyps
There are thousands of different invertebrates (animals without backbones) living in the ocean.

A coral reef is made up of lots of tiny coral polyps which live inside small chalky structures made of calcium. At feeding time they push their tentacles out to catch food floating past. Corals are invertebrates.

INVERTEBRATES

Fact 34

Soft Coral
Species of invertebrates in the ocean are corals, crabs, sea stars, sea urchins, shrimps and octopus.

Soft corals feed on particles of food floating in the seawater. Corals are sessile which means they stay in one place and let their food come to them through the water. A creature which moves around is motile – so fish which swim are motile.

INVERTEBRATES

Fact 35

Jellyfish
Different species of jellyfish and corals have been in the ocean for over 500 million years.

Jellyfish have no brains and just float around in the water eating plankton. Some have stinging tentacles. The tentacles of jellyfish get eaten by predators.

INVERTEBRATES

Fact 36

Spiny Lobster
Lobsters are crustaceans, with a shell on the outside of their body.

Lobsters have two long antennae which they push out in front of them to keep away from predators.

INVERTEBRATES

Fact 37

Giant Clam
Giant clams are bivalves – meaning they have two shells.

The two shells are hinged so they can close up tightly. Clams suck water into their bodies to extract any food. They syphon water through their bodies continuously until they feel threatened – which is when they close up the two shells so nothing can eat them.

INVERTEBRATES

Fact
38

SUPER FACT
There are more than 3000 species of sea slugs in the oceans, all with different patterns and colours.

Sea Slugs
Sea slugs are not like the slugs in your garden. They are not black and slimy.

Sea slugs do not have gills like fish so they absorb oxygen gas from the oceans through little feathery organs sticking out from their backs. Sea Slugs have a posh scientific name – nudibranchs.

Photo credit: Kris Mikael Krister on Unsplash

INVERTEBRATES

Fact
39

Sea Cucumbers
Sea Cucumbers are like a tube with seawater going through the middle.

They suck in the water to extract food, then push it out of the other end. They walk very slowly across the seabed and have large numbers of small legs. There are no bones in their bodies.

INVERTEBRATES

Fact
40

Cuttlefish
Cuttlefish are related to octopus.

They have a small bony structure in their bodies, but it is not a backbone, so they are still invertebrates.

INVERTEBRATES

Fact 41

Tube Worms

In the ocean there are worms which hide inside tubes when they feel threatened.

These worms cannot move around or run away – so they retreat into their tubes for protection.

INVERTEBRATES

Fact 42

Sea Star
Star fish are not fish – they are invertebrates and are called sea stars by scientists.

Sea stars have no blood and no brains and cannot survive in fresh water.

INVERTEBRATES

Fact 43

SUPER FACT
Scientists believe there are still 2-10 million species yet to discover living in the ocean.

Octopus
Octopus have nine brains, eight tentacles, and three hearts. Their blood is blue.

Octopus are the most amazing animals. Mostly harmless to humans ... but don't get near to a blue ringed octopus as it is so poisonous it could kill you.

HUMANS AND THE OCEANS

Fact
44

Humans and the Ocean
Humans have been using the oceans as a dumping ground.

Once you drop something in the ocean – you no longer see it. Humans brains 'see' that as the object has disappeared' but of course it hasn't disappeared – it has just become junk in the ocean which often ends up on the beach.

Photo credit: Angela Compagnone on Unsplash

HUMANS AND THE OCEANS

Fact
45

Plastic Pollution
Humans pollute the oceans with plastics, sewage, sound, oil and chemicals.

We all know about the plastics problem now and hopefully we are all looking for alternatives to using plastics. There should be an urgency to also stop polluting the oceans with raw sewage too.

Photo credit: Nataliya Vaitkevich

HUMANS AND THE OCEANS

Fact
46

Overfishing
Human are overfishing the seas. Huge super trawlers are decimating the oceans and there is likely to be very few fish in the seas by the 2030's

Can we change the system of what we eat from the oceans? Why not have farms growing algae (seaweed) which is very nutritious. Supertrawlers don't just catch fish - they catch dolphins, manta rays and turtles too - and those creatures all die when caught up in the supertrawlers nets.

Photo credit: NOAA Photo Library

HUMANS AND THE OCEANS

Fact
47

Carbon 'Sink'
Oceans have always acted as a 'carbon sink' for the planet and absorbed excess carbon dioxide produced by natural sources such as volcanoes.

We can increase the oceans' ability to capture carbon by growing more seagrass meadows around the coasts.

HUMANS AND THE OCEANS

Fact
48

Seagrass
Phytoplankton and seagrass releases 80% of oxygen to the Earth's atmosphere.

For years people have called the rain forests the 'lungs of the world' – but in fact it is oceans that supply 80% of our atmospheric oxygen, whilst the rain forests supply 20%. Let's cheer for the oceans!

HUMANS AND THE OCEANS

Fact
49

Plankton
When plankton is reproducing, it can cover vast areas of the oceans. The bright green near the surface of the oceans can be seen from space.

Plankton is not a plant, it is an algae. It is made up of microscopic algae called diatoms.

Photo credit: NASA

HUMANS AND THE OCEANS

Fact
50

SUPER FACT
Humans must stop producing carbon dioxide. If the phytoplankton and seagrass in the oceans cannot produce and release 80% oxygen to the atmosphere then all life on earth could become extinct.

Dangerous CO_2
The oceans are now full of the carbon dioxide produced by humans.

Carbon dioxide is turning to carbonic acid in the oceans, which is making the oceans acid. This acidity is killing the plankton which is supplying our oxygen.

Now read thousands of facts in 'World Beneath the Waves' book

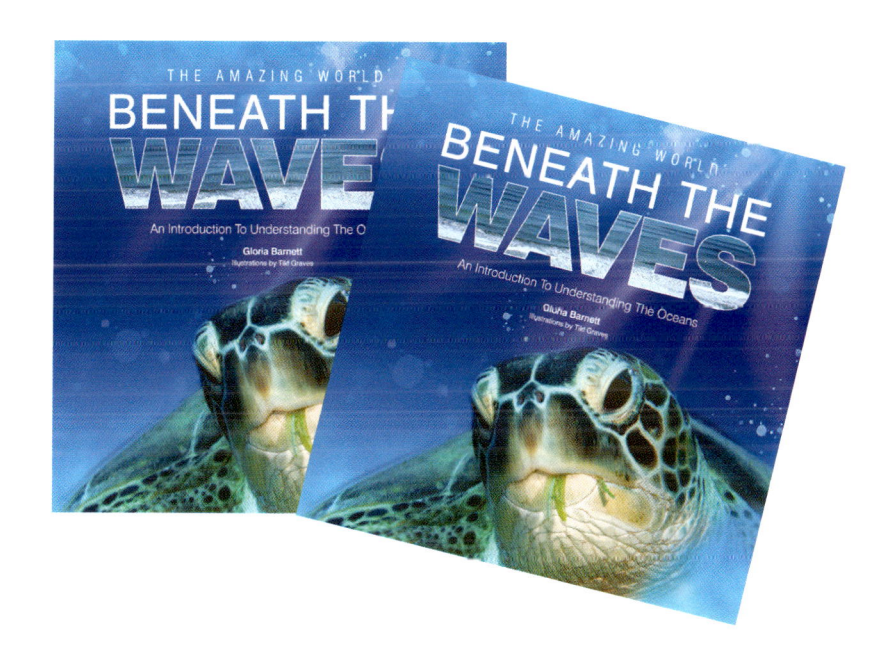

Available from: www.barnettauthor.co.uk or Amazon (worldwide)

ABOUT THE AUTHOR

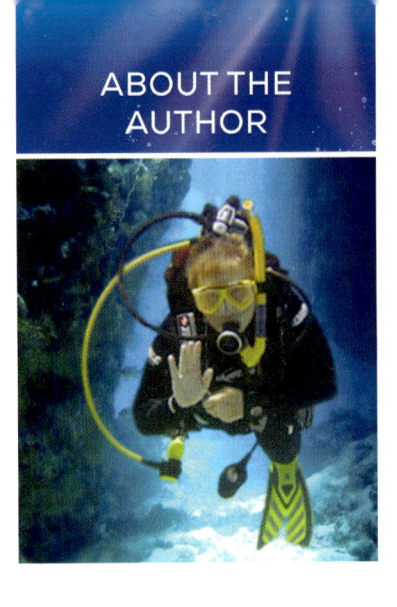

For over 30 years Gloria has been exploring our planet's oceans and has dived in a variety of areas around the world. She is a master scuba diver, keen sailor and underwater videographer as well as an educational advisor, science presenter and author.

Gloria visits schools in her guise as the 'WeirdFish Lady' presenting 'Underwater Adventure Days' to inspire and encourage learning about the natural world.

Go to www.barnettauthor.co.uk for information about Gloria's work or to subscribe to newsletters. Contact her at: gloria@barnettauthor.co.uk

Remember:
- there is only one planet Earth
- it is our home - please help to look after it!